W9-DCI-585

Beside Still Waters
Devotional

LEILA ROSE-GORDON

Besides Still Waters-Devotional © 2017
By Leila Rose- Gordon

Published by Leila Rose-Gordon, Queens, NY.
lgordon989@gmail.com

Printed by CreateSpace, An Amazon.com Company
CreateSpace, Charleston SC.

All rights reserved. No part of this publication may be reproduced, stored in a retrieval system, or transmitted in any form or by any means – electronic, mechanical, photocopying, recording, or otherwise – without the prior written permission of the publisher. The only exception is brief quotations in printed reviews.

This is a work of non-fiction. Although this is a work of non-fiction, some names, characters, places, brands, media, and incidents are products of the author's imagination and/or they are used fictitiously.

Unless otherwise identified, Scripture quotations are from the KJV Bible.

Quotes from Ellen G. White's Writings are used by permission.

Besides Still Waters-Devotional / Leila Rose-Gordon

ISBN-13: 978-1546377856
ISBN-10: 1546377859

Cover art & design: Leila Rose-Gordon
Illustrations: Pixabay.com and Pd4pic.com-Public Domain
Editors/Contributors: Dawnette Blackwood-Rhoomes and Dianna Rose
Poem © 2017 by Leila Rose-Gordon

DEDICATION

I dedicate this book to the Good Shepherd.

Table of Contents

Acknowledgements

Special thanks, first, to God, for His awesomeness. The wonder of it all, to know that God loves us, and that He created us human beings after having provided everything we needed, not just to survive, but to thrive. We were made to give Him worship, praise, and adoration, and our understanding of this truth is essential to our happiness and peace of mind.

Thanks to my family, who, from my childhood, provided the right environment for me to exult in the beauty of God's nature, and His creation. I truly believe that this atmosphere made it easy for me to experience depths of happiness that have helped to shape who I am today.

Thanks to my son Jeremy Gordon, whose love for animals helped me and my husband John Gordon to have an even deeper appreciation of God's creation, as we sought to ensure that he would always be able to see God's amazing creatures up close.

Thanks to my dear sister Dawnette Blackwood-Rhoomes, who continues this journey with me, to become all that we are in Christ and to share this discovery with the world. Thank you for sharing my love and passion for writing.

Thanks to Dianna Rose, my beloved niece. Your energy, creativity, love and passion are contagious, and have brought a new excitement to our journey.

Thanks to my readers. I hope you enjoy this book as much as I enjoy sharing it with you. If it helps you in your journey, then I am blessed beyond measure.

Introduction

Beside Still Waters takes us on a special journey that demands the engagement of your heart, mind, body and soul. It is a celebration of God's beautiful Creation and an acknowledgement of His Lordship! This trip requires reflection and self-exploration, taking us beyond the physical self to the spiritual realm where God dwells. The reader is invited to move away from the ordinary, into the extraordinary, from mere existence to the joy of living life to its fullest, as one of God's creations. We are challenged to view life differently, to face the daily challenges but at the same time make time for relaxation.

The process begins with an introduction to Jesus, God's Son-Shepherd of our lives-who is available to guide us, His sheep, daily. His presence gives meaning and purpose to our lives. The book directs us to open our hearts to the Holy Spirit who will equip us with the tools necessary to engage in spiritual warfare against the devil who is seeking to destroy us and our families. An invitation is also extended to accept the commission to share the good news of salvation with others.

The journey ultimately is one that promises success, if certain conditions have been met. It guides us to complete surrender to the will of God. Are you up to the task? Are you willing to take this journey? I am praying for you. Allow Jesus, the Son of God, and the Shepherd of the Sheep, to lead you beside still waters.

Note on how to use this book as a Devotional: Read one chapter per day and take the time to reflect on the Scripture(s) provided in the chapter. Also, write down your prayers or thoughts on the blank lines provided. Finally, seek out places and/or landscapes in which you can spend your quiet time with Him!

Reflections of the Sheep

Psalm 23

¹ The LORD is my shepherd; I shall not want.

² He maketh me to lie down in green pastures: he leadeth me beside the still waters.

³ He restoreth my soul: he leadeth me in the paths of righteousness for his name's sake.

⁴ Yea, though I walk through the valley of the shadow of death, I will fear no evil: for thou art with me; thy rod and thy staff they comfort me.

⁵ Thou preparest a table before me in the presence of mine enemies: thou anointest my head with oil; my cup runneth over.

⁶ Surely goodness and mercy shall follow me all the days of my life:
and I will dwell in the house of the LORD for ever.

When David was writing Psalm 23 he was talking about his relationship with God the Father. It is also seen as a prophetic psalm because he alludes to the long awaited Messiah-Jesus Christ, who is our Good Shepherd and Savior.

David did not know his Messiah personally because Jesus had not come into the world as a babe as yet, however, he knew that a Messiah was prophesied, and the Holy Spirit impressed upon his heart to write Psalm 23 as well as other psalms prophesying the coming of the Messiah.

In this devotional we are looking at this psalm from a prophetic perspective.

It is my prayer for you dear Reader, that you will come to know Jesus in such a way that you will be able to repeat the words of the 23rd Psalm with the full assurance of a sheep that knows his Shepherd and has complete confidence in Him!

What does the psalm mean to you? Take some time to reflect on all of God's goodness and mercy, and pen your thoughts below.

Notes

_____

_____

_____

_____

_____

_____

Beside Still Waters

Psalm 23:1-2

¹ The LORD is my shepherd; I shall not want.
*² He maketh me to lie down in green pastures: he leadeth me **beside the still waters**.*

Whenever I think of still waters I think of peace and tranquility. I think of a place that will calm my nerves. We all need a quiet place, in nature preferably, where we can find comfort, healing and restoration. We need a place where we can get away from the hustle and bustle of life and the unrelenting demands of work and duty. For example, a car gets that when we refill the tank. It gets the fuel it needs to keep moving. Resting "Beside Still Waters" is a time that is quiet, where we can be alone with Jesus; where we can meditate, and abide in Him. It is a time that is reviving, replenishing, energizing, and uplifting. It can also be an awakening; a time of revelation and enlightenment.

Picture it now-your special time with Jesus who declared in His word, the Holy Bible, "*I am the way and the truth and the life. No one comes to the Father except through me.*" (John 14:6).

Suggestion: - Take some time to focus on Jesus and get in the right frame of mind by including uplifting music or songs (your preference). You can pack a huge picnic basket and prepare yourself for some real quality time with Him.

List some of the ways you can spend quality time with Jesus.

Notes

_____

_____

_____

_____

_____

_____

_____

_____

_____

_____

_____

_____

_____

Starting the Journey

Psalm 46:10

¹⁰ Be still, and know that I am God: I will be exalted among the heathen, I will be exalted in the earth.

Location

The beach can be such a place, but make sure you stay in an area that offers the quietness and solace you need. A lake can also be appropriate. Or it can be by a pond in a nearby park, where seats are available.

Creating the scene

For those who cannot get away you can create the scene or scenery. A DVD with images of nature, with lots of water scenes and accompanying music, plus a comfortable chair or sofa which allows for relaxation and reflection, will set the right mood for you. Become a part of the scenery you have created.

Notes

The Good Shepherd-Call of Jesus

Jeremiah 31:3

³ The LORD hath appeared of old unto me, saying, Yea, I have loved thee with an everlasting love: therefore with lovingkindness have I drawn thee.

In the Holy Bible Jesus is the Good Shepherd. Let every wanderer from the fold take courage that the Good Shepherd is searching for you! Remember His work is to seek and to save that which was lost-that means me, that means you.

Jesus found me! What a beautiful day that was! He wants to find you. You are so precious to Him. Please do not run from Him all your life. Answer His call! If you want to know more about Jesus-read His Holy words as found in The Holy Bible. Look around in nature on all that God has created. You are His ultimate creation. How He loves you!

In John 3:16 it says, *For God so loved the world that He gave His only begotten Son, that whosoever believeth in Him should not perish, but have everlasting life.*

John 3:17 says, *For God sent not His Son into the world to condemn the world, but that the world through Him, might be saved.*

Be comforted by these words today.

Notes

_____

_____

_____

_____

_____

_____

_____

_____

_____

_____

_____

_____

_____

Come Home! Tarry No Longer!

Psalm 34:8

8 O taste and see that the LORD is good: blessed is the man that trusteth in him.

Year after year people struggle to move on with their lives. They find it so hard to shake off the past. They can scarcely hope in new beginnings. They feel they have gone too far, fallen too low, sunken too deep.

For others, they experienced some type of loss-the illness or death of loved ones, financial failure, divorce, separation, estrangement, unemployment, or some devastating news and they just can't seem to get over or get past the event. Their lives have been shattered.

My prayer for you, whoever you are, is that you will try the God of new beginnings. Truly His grace is sufficient, whatever ails you! But you cannot experience it unless you give over the controls of your life to Him. Simply ask Him to take over, to lead, to guide. He truly knows what is best for your life!

There is nothing in your life that is too complicated for God to handle, or to fix. You see, you can never catch Him by surprise, for He knows all your possible 'circumstances'. It does not matter how messed up you are, or how shattered or lost or hopeless you feel-God can restore you, if you are willing. Do not delay any longer! Come Home! Taste and see that the Lord is good!

Notes

I Am Tired Lord

Matthew 11:28

²⁸ Come unto me, all ye that labour and are heavy laden, and I will give you rest

Today was rough. I worked on and on and felt my body weakening under the physical and mental strain. As the day wore on, however, I was conscious of God's abiding presence. When Jesus was here on Earth He often got tired, therefore I felt good knowing that He cares for my every need, and understands How I feel.

While Jesus sojourned on this earth, He told His followers to come aside and rest awhile. He often went up into the hills to be alone with God the Father. How much more do we, sinful human beings, need to pause from our wearisome tasks and converse with God!
Matthew 11:28, 29 tells us: *Come unto me all ye that labour and are heavy laden, and I will give you rest. Take my yoke upon you, and learn of me; for I am meek and lowly in heart, and ye shall find rest unto your souls.*

As we dialogue with God, our relationship with Him will deepen, and we will grow from strength to strength. Similarly, as we study God's messages of love in His book, the Holy Bible, we will be changed from day to day into His image.

What precious promises, what comfort is found in the scriptures! Truly, Hebrews 4:12 tells us: *For the word of God is quick, and powerful, and sharper than any two-edged sword, piercing* even to the dividing *asunder of soul and spirit, and of the joints and marrow, and is a discerner of the thoughts and intents of the heart.*

Are you desirous of a closer walk with God today? Tell Him so; begin to study the bible daily; take comfort from God's precious promises, as you are reminded to do in 1 Peter 5:7, *Casting all your care upon Him, for He careth for you!*

Notes

_____

_____

_____

_____

_____

_____

_____

_____

_____

_____

_____

Shepherd Me O God

John 16:33

33 These things I have spoken unto you, that in me ye might have peace. In the world ye shall have tribulation: but be of good cheer; I have overcome the world.

PRAYER

Oh Lord, through this life, let me never forget that You are my Shepherd. Shepherd me O God, through all the vicissitudes of this life, good or bad. When you Shepherd me I find peace and rest in you.

Amen

Notes

Fountain of Living Waters

Jeremiah 2:13

¹³ For my people have committed two evils; they have forsaken me the fountain of living waters, and hewed them out cisterns, broken cisterns, that can hold no water.

Dictionary.com describes a cistern as a reservoir, tank, or container for storing or holding water or other liquid. A broken cistern indicates therefore that the water collected would run right out and no water would be able to be stored. To pour water in such a container would be a fruitless activity.

Similarly, God's people here are hopelessly trying to live a meaningful life outside of Jesus. Anything they attempt outside of Christ will ultimately fail. Like the broken cistern their lives might at times appear to be successful but in truth time will reveal that they are doomed to failure.

In John 16:5 Jesus says: *⁵ I am the vine, ye are the branches: He that abideth in me, and I in him, the same bringeth forth much fruit: for without me ye can do nothing.*

He accuses His people of forsaking Him, the fountain of living waters. This verse in Jeremiah 2:13 clearly indicates Jesus as the source of water that keeps running, that can never dry up. When we have Jesus our lives will be fruitful and we can constantly draw water from this source. Return to Him today!

Notes

_____

_____

_____

_____

_____

_____

_____

_____

_____

_____

_____

_____

_____

_____

Have Thine Own Way!

Philippians 1:6

⁶ Being confident of this very thing, that He which hath begun a good work in you will perform it until the day of Jesus Christ.

Sometimes in our walk with God we reach a point where we have no requests, where we just want to relax a little and contemplate how much He loves us. Our response to His amazing love is "Have your way!"

At these times, we somehow understand the big picture-we see so clearly that all of creation worships at His feet, and we want to do the same. We do not question His leading; we do not doubt His perfect will. We know that He will take care of our every need, that nothing happens by chance, and that everything will somehow work out in the end.

With that confidence and assurance, we step out boldly into the unknown. As surely as the sun rises and sets in our part of the world, we know that we can count on Him to complete His work in us.

That assurance brings us peace and comfort even during trials and tribulations. And so, we go forward in His name, claiming His wondrous promises, conquering our fears, and making huge strides in our spiritual journey.

We celebrate these times when they come, and we do not take them for granted. They are the occasional oasis in our desert experience. Soon we begin to understand more and more, and we begin to make wiser choices that lead to streams, and more frequent rest stops.

We make less haste, calm takes the place of anxiety, and earth becomes a heavenly experience, an abiding. We dwell in the presence of God. May that mountaintop experience be yours today-it begins when we decide to let God have His way!

Notes

Wait on the Lord

Isaiah 40:28-31

*[28] Hast thou not known? hast thou not heard, that the everlasting
God, the Lord, the Creator of the ends of the earth, fainteth not,
neither is weary? there is no searching of his understanding.
[29] He giveth power to the faint; and to them that have no might he
increaseth strength.
[30] Even the youths shall faint and be weary, and the young men shall
utterly fall;
[31] But they that wait upon the Lord shall renew their strength; they
shall mount up with wings as eagles; they shall run, and not be
weary; and they shall walk, and not faint.*

There will be times when we will become tired physically, mentally,
spiritually and emotionally, but we can always claim God's promise
of power and strength to re-energize us for our journey.

The Bible, the word of God, has such precious promises and
assurances to help us on our daily walk of faith. I am so grateful that

we have not been left comfortless in these perilous times in which we live.

PRAYER

Dear Lord, whatever our struggles today, teach us to wait on You, to trust and to put our all in You, knowing that You care for us, and will provide for us daily. It is so reassuring to know that You understand and will never grow weary. We love You Lord. Please give us the power and strength that we need to be victorious today. Thank You in advance for answering our prayers.

Amen.

Notes

_____

_____

_____

_____

_____

_____

_____

_____

_____

_____

_____

God Has Great Plans for Your Life

Jeremiah 29:11 (New American Standard version)

11 'For I know the plans that I have for you,' declares the LORD, 'plans for welfare and not for calamity to give you a future and a hope.'

Whatever your desert experience today, it will not last! Be excited with the knowledge that God's promises are sure. Claim His promise of a bright future. He has great plans for your life and one day that desert experience will have to give way to the oasis! In my own life I have come to realize that I wouldn't appreciate the oasis periods in my life if I didn't go through the desert.

A precious bible promise is found in John 10:10, where Jesus says, *10 The thief cometh not, but for to steal, and to kill, and to destroy: I am come that they might have life, and that they might have it more abundantly.*

Notes

God's Rest Stops

Isaiah 40:29

²⁹ He giveth power to the faint; and to them that have no might he increaseth strength.

Recently I have been learning to take advantage of God's rest stops. Life can get very busy. Sometimes twenty-four hours just seem to be inadequate to get through all the obligations you must meet daily. There is so much to be done, so much to accomplish. It can become so hectic that your nerves begin to scream for release. Outwardly you might be able to maintain your composure but inwardly you feel as if you are losing your grip.

So how do you get a grip? How can you see life as you once saw it, in positive terms, full of hope and eagerly looking toward the future?

Friend, you must check out God's rest stops. Do not take these for granted. Do not wave them aside when they come. They will come. Life is designed that way so that you remain sane-really! So, the next time you receive an invitation to go to a picnic, or a get-together, or play a game, or some other form of meaningful entertainment, do not look for an excuse.

Remember the work will always be there. You must come to the point where you also value leisure, where you place it in your busy schedule. You would be amazed how it relaxes the mind and repairs frazzled nerves.

When last did you go to a beach, and just let your toes curl over the pebbles in the sand, and let the water lap across your feet? Try it. It is so invigorating, so relaxing, calming, soothing, and healing! Allow yourself to feel at one with nature, God's world. Feel the stress, the weariness, and the anxiety leaving your body. You will come away from the experience rejuvenated, ready to take on tomorrow's challenges.

Breaks-especially ones that give you a chance to focus on God as Creator-help you to put life's challenges in proper perspective. You will find that you are better able physically, mentally and spiritually to cope with them when they come.

Notes

_____

_____

_____

_____

_____

_____

_____

_____

Don't Worry-Be Happy

Philippians 4:6, 7 & 8

6 Be careful for nothing: but in everything by prayer and supplication with thanksgiving let your requests be made known unto God.
7 And the peace of God, which passeth all understanding, shall keep your hearts and minds through Christ Jesus.
8 Finally, brethren, whatsoever things are true, whatsoever things are honest, whatsoever things are just, whatsoever things are pure, whatsoever things are lovely, whatsoever things are of good report: if there be any virtue, and if there be any praise, think on these things.

Let this text comfort you daily, more and more as you see the day approaching. This is a great way to avoid stress building up in your body. When we dwell too much on the cares of life we often become overwhelmed, burdened, anxious and even depressed. Over time too much stress can lead to hypertension, heart disease, diabetes and other ailments.

Instead of worrying about our problems God is asking us to hand them over to Him. In return He gives us His peace. What a wonderful exchange!

Notes

_____

_____

_____

_____

_____

_____

_____

_____

_____

_____

_____

_____

_____

_____

New Beginnings

2 Corinthians 3:18

18 But we all, with open face beholding as in a glass the glory of the Lord, are changed into the same image from glory to glory, even as by the Spirit of the Lord.

Do not despair! There is always time for new beginnings. Whether you are young or old, with God, there are no failures. Start anew. Keep hope alive in your heart.

Psalm 119:9 states: *9 Wherewithal shall a young man cleanse his way? By taking heed thereto according to Thy word.*

John 3:16, 17 tells of God's love for the world. *16 For God so loved the world, that He gave his only begotten Son, that whosoever believeth in Him should not perish, but have everlasting life. 17 For*

God sent not his Son into the world to condemn the world; but that the world through Him might be saved.

That means you, that means me. He gave, and He has not stopped giving. What will your response be to Him today? If you are not sure where to start, why not whisper a prayer in your heart. Ask God, from today, to lead your life. Ask Him from today, to be Lord of your life.

You might feel that the picture you have been painting is marred, that there is no hope for beauty, nothing to admire in the ugly, runny colors that you dashed across the page called your life. Give the canvas back to Him, and let Him teach you how to paint beautiful colors. Let Him paint a portrait of you that will be a joy to others. Let Him give your life true meaning, and purpose.

Then stand back and admire His handiwork. Truly from the beginning, what He saw was good. Let Him recreate that image of you that will make you stand tall and proud.

You can do it, but you cannot do it by yourself. Take that leap of faith today. Let go, and let God!

Notes

_____

_____

_____

_____

_____

_____

_____

_____

The Way Home

Psalm 1

¹ Blessed is the man that walketh not in the counsel of the ungodly, nor standeth in the way of sinners, nor sitteth in the seat of the scornful.

² But his delight is in the law of the LORD; and in his law doth he meditate day and night.

³ And he shall be like a tree planted by the rivers of water, that bringeth forth his fruit in his season; his leaf also shall not wither; and whatsoever he doeth shall prosper.

⁴ The ungodly are not so: but are like the chaff which the wind driveth away.

⁵ Therefore the ungodly shall not stand in the judgment, nor sinners in the congregation of the righteous.

⁶ For the LORD knoweth the way of the righteous: but the way of the ungodly shall perish.

Study this Psalm. Hide the words in your heart. Delight in the law of the Lord and you will see these precious promises come to pass in your life!

Notes

_____

_____

_____

_____

_____

_____

_____

_____

_____

_____

_____

_____

_____

_____

_____

_____

Let God Lead You!

Psalm 139: 23 & 24

²³ Search me, O God, and know my heart: try me, and know my thoughts:

²⁴ And see if there be any wicked way in me, and lead me in the way everlasting.

I thought I was in the basement, but I wasn't! I woke up suddenly, startled, needing to use the bathroom. I was still in my son's room where I had fallen asleep after praying with him.

The room in the basement is one of my quiet places, my sanctuary, where I can talk with God quietly and pen my thoughts. I had not reached my destination.

In the same way, you might think that you are headed in the right direction in your life, but that might be far from the case.

Hand over the controls of your life to God, and let Him lead you home.

Don't even try to go any further on your own. Just stop. Like the GPS system God can recalculate the directions and turn you in the direction you should have been going. Yes, He is calling you home. Listen to Him!

Notes

_____

_____

_____

_____

_____

_____

_____

_____

_____

_____

_____

_____

_____

_____

The Paths of Righteousness

Psalm 23:3

...He leadeth me in the paths of righteousness for His name sake.

Let Him take care of the details of your life. He will guide you along the best paths for your life, the paths of righteousness. Even if you are walking through the Valley of the Shadow of Death you need fear no evil. His promise is that He will be with you and His rod and His staff will comfort you. Put all your trust in Him. He is faithful to His promise.

In Psalm 37:4-7 we are given this beautiful promise: *4Delight thyself also in the LORD; and He shall give thee the desires of thine heart. 5Commit thy way unto the LORD; trust also in Him; and He shall bring it to pass. 6And He shall bring forth thy righteousness as the light, and thy judgment as the noonday.*

Also in 1 Peter 5:7 we are given a wonderful reason why we should depend on Jesus: *7 Casting all your care upon him; for he careth for you.*

Notes

_____

_____

_____

_____

_____

_____

_____

_____

_____

_____

_____

_____

_____

_____

_____

_____

_____

Cleansed and Renewed

Hebrews 10:22

²² Let us draw near with a true heart in full assurance of faith, having our hearts sprinkled from an evil conscience, and our bodies washed with pure water.

What a blessed assurance! We can start again, knowing that all our sins have been washed away. With our past and all our failures and shortcomings behind us, we can face the future confidently knowing that Jesus will lead us all the way!

Although the Christian will always be faced with trials and temptations in this life, remember that we will not be fighting this spiritual battle on our own. We can be victorious through Jesus Christ.

In 1 John 2:1 we are told: *¹My little children, these things write I unto you, that ye sin not. And if any man sin, we have an advocate with the Father, Jesus Christ the righteous:*

God wants us to put Him first in our lives. We must be careful not to allow anything or anyone to take His place. Whatever comes between us and God becomes our idol. It will never bring the satisfaction we seek. Let us surrender to Him completely.

Ezekiel 36:25 says, *25 Then will I sprinkle clean water upon you, and ye shall be clean from all your filthiness, and from all your idols, will I cleanse you.*

Let us trust in our Creator to know what is best for our lives. Claim His precious promises. Place your confidence in Him!

Notes

_____

_____

_____

_____

_____

_____

_____

_____

_____

_____

_____

_____

Newness of Life-Holy Spirit

John 3:5

⁵ Jesus answered, Verily, verily, I say unto thee, Except a man be born of water and of the Spirit, he cannot enter into the kingdom of God.

In John 7:38, 39 Jesus said, *³⁸ He that believeth on me, as the scripture hath said, out of his belly shall flow rivers of living water.*

³⁹ (But this spake He of the Spirit, which they that believe on Him should receive: for the Holy Ghost was not yet given; because that Jesus was not yet glorified.)

In John 14:16-17 Jesus tells His disciples, *¹⁶ And I will pray the Father, and He shall give you another Comforter, that He may abide with you forever; ¹⁷ Even the Spirit of truth; whom the world cannot receive, because it seeth Him not, neither knoweth Him: but ye know Him; for He dwelleth with you, and shall be in you.*

Jesus fulfilled His promise to His disciples because on the Day of Pentecost while they were gathered together they received the Holy Spirit. We are told in Acts 2:4 that *they were all filled with the Holy Ghost, and began to speak with other tongues, as the Spirit gave them utterance.* As a result, they were able to witness to and baptize three thousand souls that day. As Peter explained to the crowd that had gathered to listen, this same Holy Spirit is available to us today.

In Acts 2:38 & 39 he said, *38 Repent, and be baptized every one of you in the name of Jesus Christ for the remission of sins, and ye shall receive the gift of the Holy Ghost.*

39 For the promise is unto you, and to your children, and to all that are *afar off, even as many as the LORD our God shall call.*

That promise includes us living in the present age! How wonderful! In Luke 11:13 Jesus also assured us of this. *13 If ye then, being evil, know how to give good gifts unto your children: how much more shall your heavenly Father give the Holy Spirit to them that ask Him?*

My Friends, read this account for yourself in God's Holy Word, the Bible, and if you have not already done so, accept this clear invitation from Jesus to believe in Him. Then you too can walk in newness of life!

Notes

Quenching Your Thirst

John 4:14

[14] But whosoever drinketh of the water that I shall give him shall never thirst; but the water that I shall give him shall be in him a well of water springing up into everlasting life.

Jesus has issued the invitation in different ways, for us to believe in Him and accept Him and be saved from our sins. The penalty of sin, which is death and eternal separation from God, has been paid by Jesus who took our place and died for our sins. He lives again and intercedes for us, offering us His righteousness. When we accept His offer we will have newness of life. He will make available to us His Holy Spirit who will give us power to be victorious over sin. The Holy Spirit in our lives also transforms us into God's image.

In Galations 5:22-23 we are told, *[22] But the fruit of the Spirit is love, joy, peace, longsuffering, gentleness, goodness, faith, [23] Meekness, temperance: against such there is no law.*

Jesus also said in John 6:39-40: *39 And this is the Father's will which hath sent me, that of all which he hath given me I should lose nothing, but should raise it up again at the last day. 40 And this is the will of Him that sent me, that every one which seeth the Son, and believeth on Him, may have everlasting life: and I will raise him up at the last day.*

This is good news. Although we may die physically before His return, the blessed hope is that one day when Jesus comes back for us (who allowed His Spirit to transform us into God's image) we will be resurrected and we will be with Him for eternity.

In 1 Thessalonians 4:17 we are told *17 Then we which are alive and remain shall be caught up together with them in the clouds, to meet the Lord in the air: and so shall we ever be with the Lord.*

Notes

_____

_____

_____

_____

_____

_____

_____

_____

_____

_____

_____

Promise of Blessings

Isaiah 44:3

³ For I will pour water upon him that is thirsty, and floods upon the dry ground: I will pour My spirit upon thy seed, and My blessing upon thine offspring:

The promise of the Holy Spirit is to help us sojourn this life successfully. The success I speak of is not as men count success. God has a plan and a purpose for our lives. We are not on Earth by chance. In Jeremiah 1:5 we are told: *⁵ Before I formed thee in the belly I knew thee; and before thou camest forth out of the womb I sanctified thee, and I ordained thee a prophet unto the nations.*

The Holy Spirit will be your guide. You will not be alone. John 16:13 tells us: *¹³ Howbeit when He, the Spirit of truth, is come, He will guide you into all truth: for He shall not speak of Himself; but whatsoever He shall hear, that shall He speak: and He will shew you things to come.* Do not hesitate to ask Jesus for this precious gift of the Holy Spirit today!

Notes

Protected

Isaiah 49:10

¹⁰ They shall not hunger nor thirst; neither shall the heat nor sun smite them: for He that hath mercy on them shall lead them, even by the springs of water shall He guide them.

Trust in God to take care of you. When you accept God's call you cannot continue to depend upon yourself. Jesus will guide you. He has gone to Heaven and He has told us He is preparing a place for us. He wants us to be with Him. Until that time comes He will be our guide and protector. In John 14:6 Jesus answered, *⁶ I am the way and the truth and the life. No one comes to the Father except through me.*

But while we wait, there is something He is asking us to do, as outlined in Ephesians 6:11-18: *¹¹Put on the whole armour of God, that ye may be able to stand against the wiles of the devil. ¹² For we wrestle not against flesh and blood, but against principalities, against powers, against the rulers of the darkness of this world, against spiritual wickedness in high places. ¹³ Wherefore take unto* *you the whole armour of God, that ye may be able to withstand in the evil day, and having done all, to stand. 14 Stand therefore, having your loins girt about with truth, and having on the breastplate of righteousness; 15 And your feet shod with the preparation of the gospel of peace; 16 Above all, taking the shield of faith, wherewith ye shall be able to quench all the fiery darts of the wicked. 17 And take the helmet of salvation, and the sword of the Spirit, which is the word of God: 18 Praying always with all prayer and supplication in the Spirit, and watching thereunto with all perseverance and supplication for all saints."*

We are admonished to study God's written word daily as the Bible is His roadmap or guidebook for us to reach our destination safely. As we study His word we come to know more about God the Father, God the Son (Jesus, the living Word who leads the way-John 1:1-34) and God, the Holy Spirit.

In response to the study of God's word we seek to obey His commands. We are encouraged to have a strong prayer life as it is through prayer that we communicate with God and make our requests known to Him. It is also through prayer that we gain strength to obey God and live in accordance with His will. In Hebrews 4:16 we are told: *16 Let us therefore come boldly unto the throne of grace, that we may obtain mercy, and find grace to help in time of need.*

We will receive strength from God to withstand temptations and overcome obstacles. This includes strength to resist the temptation to veer off the path of righteousness.

Finally, God asks us to share with others what we have learned from Him so that they too can receive His gift of salvation. As a result, we pray not only for ourselves but for others as well.

Notes

Quieting the Storms Within

Isaiah 12:2-3

² Behold, God is my salvation; I will trust, and not be afraid: for the LORD JEHOVAH is my strength and my song; he also is become my salvation.

³ Therefore with joy shall ye draw water out of the wells of salvation.

How do you quiet the storms within? The same way you quiet the storms that rage around you. Be still and know that He is God. Jesus is Lord over all storms. He is Lord of all. Physical storms cannot last in His presence. Neither can spiritual storms.

When we acknowledge His might and His power, when we acknowledge His leadership over our lives, then we will have the faith to believe that He can free us not only from the storms that rage without, but also from the storms that rage within.

We must talk to Him. We must ask Him to take complete control over our lives. Jesus does not want parts of us-He wants all of us!

What storms rage within that you wish to lay before Him? He will quiet them for you!

Notes

Storms From Our Perception of Life

Jeremiah 17:9
*⁹ The heart is deceitful above all things, and desperately wicked:
who can know it?*

Wrong thoughts and wrong thinking create a huge percentage of the storms that build up in our lives. Some of these storms can become tsunamis if we do not keep them in check.

Cast your cares upon God because He cares for you. Recognize that you do not know or understand everything happening around you. A lot of our beliefs are based upon faulty or false premises. Let the Holy Spirit teach us how to discern the truth.

Let us also learn how to communicate effectively with others. Often when there is dialogue we discover that the person we believe wronged us had a different intent. We must be careful, therefore, not to jump to conclusions, especially when we have not asked pertinent questions about the subject matter.

There are reasons why we are commanded not to judge others, lest we be judged. It is a very dangerous practice and one that is practiced by many. Convinced that they are right in their judgments many act rashly, jumping to conclusions based on what they presume to be facts and handing out verdict and sentencing immediately. Let us recognize that the power of discernment comes from God and is often the work of a lifetime. Recognize too that you can be wrong about someone or something and be humble in your approach, especially when engaged in heated discussions.

Give yourself the opportunity to think things through. Ask for time to reflect. Then seek the Lord earnestly for truth. The enemy of souls delights in bearing false witness and displaying falsehood as truth. Do not become his agent of destruction and disunity. Question your own thoughts and motives with due diligence.

In past events, have you offended anyone based on conclusions you have drawn about them? Ask God to give you the opportunity to right this wrong.

Notes

_____

_____

_____

_____

_____

_____

_____

_____

_____

_____

Blessed are the Peacemakers-Amidst the Storm

Matthew 5:9

⁹ Blessed are the peacemakers: for they shall be called the children of God.

Be determined to be a peacemaker in your home, your community, your workplace, your school, your church, wherever you go. Become an agent of change. With Christ in you, you will find that you too can still the storms that rage without and within.

Learn about the power of forgiveness. Love truly covers a multitude of sins. You don't have to have the last word. Learn to walk away. Learn to hold back hot words. Sit at the feet of Jesus and ask Him to give you His temperament, His character.

Replace strife and discord with unity and peace. As far as possible live peaceably with all men. *"Depart from evil, and do good; seek peace and pursue it."* (Psalm 34:14).

Notes

Storms From Being Fearful

Isaiah 41:10

[10] Fear thou not; for I am with thee: be not dismayed; for I am thy God: I will strengthen thee; yea, I will help thee; yea, I will uphold thee with the right hand of my righteousness.

Replace fear with faith! Recognize that the God of the universe can provide for your every need. He is in control and He wants you to trust Him. Worrying about issues in your life is a response that you have learned over the years. Ask God to replace this response with faith in Him and His ability to get you through this or any circumstance in your life.

Learn to live in the moment, instead of borrowing problems that you perceive could occur an hour from now or a day from now. Do not take on these problems because that is not your job. Your job is to have faith in the Problem Solver. Stand still and see the salvation of the Lord!

Whenever we find ourselves worrying or becoming full of fear we must recognize that these are choices that we make. Choose trust, choose faith! Over time they will become automatic responses as we learn to abide in Christ.

Notes

_____

_____

_____

_____

_____

_____

_____

_____

_____

_____

_____

_____

_____

_____

_____

So Send I You

John 20:21

21 Then said Jesus to them again, Peace be unto you: as My Father hath sent Me, even so send I you.

As you spend-quiet moments with God it is also a time to focus on mission. Sometimes life gets so busy we find it difficult to focus on God's call. Yet, during life's trials and tribulations, during uncertainty and turmoil, God calls us to be His missionaries. God is calling me, and He is calling you dear reader, to service.

He offers us much needed peace and at the same time He reminds us of our mission. It is so easy to become distracted, and believe me; the distractions are many and varied. Yet it is comforting to know that if we submit to His will, and we ask that His will be done on Earth as it is in Heaven, then He hears us and is ready, willing and able to grant our request. Contemplate the call of Jesus today. It is my fervent hope that you will eagerly follow where He leads!

The Bible tells us in Matthew 10:42, *"And whosoever shall give to drink unto one of these little ones a cup of cold water only in the name of a disciple, verily I say unto you, he shall in no wise lose his reward."*

In John 21:15-17 Jesus asked His disciple Peter a very pertinent question, then He gave him a command. I direct this question to you dear Reader and to me: *15 So when they had dined, Jesus saith to Simon Peter, Simon, son of Jonas, lovest thou me more than these? He saith unto him, Yea, Lord; thou knowest that I love thee. He saith unto him, Feed my lambs. 16 He saith to him again the second time, Simon, son of Jonas, lovest thou me? He saith unto him, Yea, Lord; thou knowest that I love thee. He saith unto him, Feed my sheep. 17 He saith unto him the third time, Simon, son of Jonas, lovest thou me? Peter was grieved because he said unto him the third time, Lovest thou me? And he said unto him, Lord, thou knowest all things; thou knowest that I love thee. Jesus saith unto him, Feed my sheep."*

Reach out to someone today! Help someone even in some small way. A smile, a word of encouragement-you just never know how many candles can be lit, from the spark you give. Someone may be inspired to hold onto their dreams. Someone may be inspired to give life a second try. Someone may be inspired to seek out love, seek out truth, and look for the path to a life more abundant.

Notes

_____

_____

_____

_____

_____

_____

_____

_____

_____

The Water of Life

Revelation 22:17

¹⁷ And the Spirit and the bride say, Come. And let him that heareth say, Come. And let him that is athirst come. And whosoever will, let him take the water of life freely.

Ellen G. White's Writings, **"That I May Know Him, page 98 – Christ's Blessings Universal, April 2**," reads as follows:

That was the true Light, which lighteth every man that cometh into the world. (John 1:9).

The grace of Christ is not confined to a few. The message of mercy and forgiveness brought from heaven by Christ was to be heard by all. Our Saviour says, "I am the light of the world." (John 8:12). His blessings are universal, reaching to all nations, kindreds, tongues, and peoples. Christ came to break down every wall of partition ... that every soul, whether Jew or Gentile, might be a free worshiper and have access to God....

Through varied channels the heavenly messengers are in active communication with every part of the world, and when man calls upon the Lord with a true and earnest heart, God is represented as bending from His throne above. He listens to every yearning cry, and answers, "Here am I." He raises up the distressed and oppressed. He bestows His blessings on the evil as well as on the good.

In every precept that Christ taught, He was expounding His own life. God's holy law was magnified in this living representative. He was the revealer of the infinite mind. He uttered no uncertain sentiments or opinions, but pure and holy truth.... He invites men to take a close view of God in Himself, in the infinite love therein expressed.[2] **(The Youth's Instructor, July 29, 1897).**

To know God is the most wonderful knowledge that men can have. There is much wisdom with worldly men, but with all their wisdom they behold not the beauty and majesty, the justice and wisdom, the goodness and holiness, of the Creator of all worlds. The Lord walks among men by His providences, but His stately steppings are not heard, His presence is not discerned, His hand is not recognized. The work of Christ's disciples is to shine as lights, making manifest to the world the character of God. They are to catch the increasing rays of light from the Word of God and reflect them to men enshrouded in the darkness of misapprehension of God. The servants of Christ must rightly represent the character of God and Christ to men.[3] **(The Review and Herald, March 5, 1891).**

Notes

_____

_____

_____

_____

_____

_____

_____

_____

_____

Beside Still Waters

We have one life to live then a judgment
Yet we cling to this one with all its allurements
Denying the power of the Cross
We live as if we are lost

So lead me Lord beside still waters
Speak to me of your love and power
Let me gaze upon the beauty
of Thy creation in this hour

Oh how I long to see Your face
And to leave these trials behind
Nature speaks to me of wonders
You have bestowed upon mankind

Oh take the pain and take the sadness
Take the troubles and cares of life
Give me dear Lord a heart of gladness
Forgive my sins and give me Christ

Now that I've seen Thy awesome wonders
And your Truth Lord now embraced
I'll share this message this world o'er
Of forgiveness, love and grace

Just trust His lead and gladly follow
Beside still waters you soon will be
When you give Him your tomorrows
You'll receive His blessings and He'll set you free.

by Leila Rose-Gordon
© 2017

Notes

Psalm 34

[1] I will bless the LORD at all times: his praise shall continually be in my mouth.

[2] My soul shall make her boast in the LORD: the humble shall hear thereof, and be glad.

[3] O magnify the LORD with me, and let us exalt his name together.

[4] I sought the LORD, and he heard me, and delivered me from all my fears.

[5] They looked unto him, and were lightened: and their faces were not ashamed.

[6] This poor man cried, and the LORD heard him, and saved him out of all his troubles.

[7] The angel of the LORD encampeth round about them that fear him, and delivereth them.

[8] O taste and see that the LORD is good: blessed is the man that

trusteth in him.

⁹ O fear the LORD, ye his saints: for there is no want to them that fear him.

¹⁰ The young lions do lack, and suffer hunger: but they that seek the LORD shall not want any good thing.

¹¹ Come, ye children, hearken unto me: I will teach you the fear of the LORD.

¹² What man is he that desireth life, and loveth many days, that he may see good?

¹³ Keep thy tongue from evil, and thy lips from speaking guile.

¹⁴ Depart from evil, and do good; seek peace, and pursue it.

¹⁵ The eyes of the LORD are upon the righteous, and his ears are open unto their cry.

¹⁶ The face of the LORD is against them that do evil, to cut off the remembrance of them from the earth.

¹⁷ The righteous cry, and the LORD heareth, and delivereth them out of all their troubles.

¹⁸ The LORD is nigh unto them that are of a broken heart; and saveth such as be of a contrite spirit.

¹⁹ Many are the afflictions of the righteous: but the LORD delivereth him out of them all.

²⁰ He keepeth all his bones: not one of them is broken.

²¹ Evil shall slay the wicked: and they that hate the righteous shall be desolate.

²² The LORD redeemeth the soul of his servants: and none of them that trust in him shall be desolate.

Notes

John 10:10

"¹⁰The thief cometh not, but for to steal, and to kill, and to destroy: I am come that they might have life, and that they might have it more abundantly."

Let us choose to live life and live it more abundantly in Christ Jesus, our Good Shepherd, who leads us beside still waters!

43967395R00052

Made in the USA
Middletown, DE
24 May 2017